ALL THE BEST SALADS

ALL THE BEST

SALADS

BY

JOIE WARNER

Published in Canada by

Stoddart Publishing Co. Limited
34 Lesmill Road
Don Mills, Ontario M3B 2T6

CANADIAN CATALOGING IN PUBLICATION DATA
Warner, Joie.
    All the best salads
Includes index.
ISBN 0-7737-5624-8
1. Salads.   I. Title.
TX740.W37   1994   641.8'3   C93-095339-8

Printed in the United States of America
10 9 8 7 6 5 4 3 2 1

This book was created and produced by

Flavor Publications, Inc.
208 East 51st Street, Suite 240
New York, New York 10022

ACKNOWLEDGMENTS

SPECIAL THANKS to my dear friend Kristina Goodwin of Savouries Catering for her recipes: Hearts of Palm, Baby Corn, Artichoke, and Radicchio Salad; Cantaloupe Pomegranate Salad; Lobster Salad with Lime Mayonnaise and Pink Peppercorns; and Wild and White Rice Salad with Orange Zest, Currants, and Coconut.

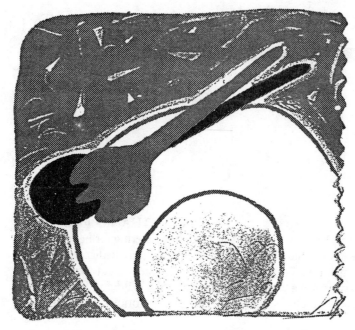

salad servers
& bowl

CONTENTS

INTRODUCTION

Time was, a salad was nothing more than a lettuce-tomato-cucumber combination drenched in a cloying bottled dressing. No more. Today's salads — infinitely more varied and innovative — have been elevated to high-art status, with chefs and home cooks using all sorts of hitherto esoteric and exotic ingredients in visually striking ways. With the rediscovery of fresh vegetables and with such an incredible range of quality salad components now available at greengrocers, specialty shops, and supermarkets, it's no wonder that cooks everywhere are turning over a new leaf. We are now tossing together healthier, tastier mixtures of gutsy greens (or no greens at all), fresh herbs, edible flowers, all manner of fish, fowl, meats, pastas, grains, nuts, legumes, eggs, and fruits with light and appealing or boldly seasoned salad dressings.

Not surprisingly, our passion for salads runs parallel to our concern with good nutrition and lighter eating. Leafy greens add important vitamins and minerals such as iron, calcium, and vitamins C and A, not to mention trace elements and fiber. (Just remember, there are more nutrients — especially vitamin A — in the darker greens.) And if other ingredients are included, such as fresh fish, vegetables, grains, dried beans, or pasta, even more nutritional punch is added to the salad bowl.

Happily, most salads are not too filling or fattening; but besides their healthy appeal, they are unbelievably quick and easy to make. These perfect spur-of-the-moment dishes need little culinary wizardry; just a good eye and the ability to choose the freshest seasonal produce. After all, if the tomatoes are not at their peak or the greens are wilted, there is no point in making a salad. And of course the perfect finishing touch is a skillfully prepared dressing using the finest oils, vinegars, and seasonings. Also keep in mind seasonal harmonies of color, shape, texture, and flavor when composing a salad.

Much more than a simple side dish, salads make wonderful appetizers, great change-of-pace entrées, first courses, light meals, lunches, palate refreshers, even desserts. A salad can be a simple plate of the tenderest greens splashed with a light vinaigrette or a substantial main-course meal chock-full of meats and vegetables. The most versatile of foods, salads can be created from virtually anything edible – either raw or cooked ingredients (they are the perfect vehicle for leftovers) or a combination – and although most salads are served cold, many are served hot or room-temperature. Moreover, they can (and should) be served at any time of the year, not just in the summertime.

All the Best Salads and Salad Dressings has the perfect salad for your menu. Here you will find salads suitable for family dinners, lunches, and more formal occasions. Recipes include classics like Caesar Salad, Salade Niçoise, and Tabbouleh along with new creations such as Four Greens with Grilled Brie or Stilton and Duck Salad with Warm Sesame Dressing. Many can be made ahead and all are easy to prepare. While many recipes seem best suited as refreshing summertime dishes because of seasonal produce, you will find many that are satisfying and hearty enough for winter meals.

Chapter one includes salad dressings ranging from the classic vinaigrette and its variations to creamy and zesty preparations. As well, most of the salads are paired with their own dressings, which you can use on salads of your own creation. The second chapter includes vegetable salads, such as popular cole slaw and potato salad, along with many that take advantage of seasonal ingredients. The third section serves up refreshing fruit salad recipes ideal for appetizers and desserts. The remaining chapters feature both hearty and light recipes based on meats, poultry, fish, and seafood and earthy pasta, beans, rice, and grain salads. Also included is a glossary of greens and lettuces, with notes on ingredients and equipment.

Few dishes offer greater possibilities for creative improvisation. So feel free to improvise. With a well-stocked pantry, an assemblage of fresh greens or vegetables, and perhaps some leftover poultry or fish, a salad can become the most satisfying part of your meal, if not one of the glories of your table.

JOIE WARNER

B A S I C S

BUYING AND PREPARING THE GREENS

Most greens can be found in greengrocers and in ethnic neighborhoods, and some "exotic" greens such as radicchio, arugula, and "baby" greens are beginning to appear in many markets and specialty food shops.

When buying greens, look for fresh, crisp, bright-colored leaves and avoid any that are discolored or have yellowing leaves. Handle all greens gently. Put unwashed greens into plastic bags, store in the refrigerator, and use as soon as possible.

The greens must be washed and dried carefully before using. Separate leaves and wash each one under gently running cold water. Certain greens like spinach and dandelions need to be rinsed — dunked up and down — in a sink full of cold water to rid them of trapped sand. Never soak greens in water or many nutrients will leach out. To dry greens, either use a salad spinner or blot the individual leaves with paper towels to remove excess moisture. The greens must be absolutely dry before adding dressing or the moisture will dilute the flavor of the dressing. Place the dried leaves in a plastic bag and store in the refrigerator to crisp and chill for as much as up to 24 hours ahead. If storing for longer than just a few hours though, it is best to layer paper towels between leaves to absorb moisture.

How to Dress a Salad

There are endless dressing possibilities, but in most instances the dressing is either a simple oil-and-vinegar (or lemon) vinaigrette or a mayonnaise dressing. These can be varied infinitely by the additions of herbs, spices, and flavorings. Other dressings are based on dairy products such as heavy or sour cream, buttermilk, yogurt, or cheese. This type is higher in protein and can be lower in calories if low-fat products are used.

The success of every salad depends largely upon the dressing because a well-prepared, properly seasoned dressing binds the various ingredients of a salad into a coherent whole. My feeling about dressings is the same as my feeling about salads: the simpler the better. Dressings that are too complex overpower the salad greens. I think the best dressing is made with a good olive oil, lemon juice, Dijon-style mustard, salt, and pepper. I might add some minced garlic, fresh or dried herbs, add a shot of hot sauce, or splash in some fruit or balsamic vinegar to enliven it even more. But a delicious dressing can only come about if the best-quality ingredients — olive oils, wine vinegars, and mustards, for example — are used. Only freshly squeezed lemon or fruit juices, fresh garlic, freshly ground pepper, and good-quality condiments, herbs, and spices will guarantee the best flavor.

The classic proportions of oil to vinegar are 3 to 1, but these elements are often varied to suit individual tastes and to complement the particular character of the greens. Pungent greens such as romaine, escarole, arugula, and spinach demand robust dressings, while delicate lettuces such as Boston or bibb are easily overpowered by stronger dressings.

Most dressings should be made just prior to tossing the salad. Some cooks prepare the dressing about a half-hour before tossing to allow the flavors to meld, but it shouldn't be made too far in advance. And since most dressings do not keep well, it is best to make them in small batches.

Whatever dressing you choose, remember, too, that you shouldn't dress a salad until just before serving or it will become limp and soggy. And never drown your salad. Use only half the dressing called for in my recipes, then toss (or rather, turn ingredients in an up-and-over motion), and add more dressing if insufficient. Also, it is difficult to advise as to the precise amounts of dressing for each salad because heads of lettuce and other greens vary in size. You may also have to add a little more oil, vinegar, and seasonings to a salad for this reason.

You must mix the salad ingredients gently with your hands or salad servers so that you do not bruise the leaves. Choose a very large bowl for tossing or your salad ingredients will constantly be flying out of the bowl and they won't be adequately coated with dressing.

Lastly, if you must prepare everything ahead of time, pour the dressing into bottom of salad bowl, place greens lightly on top (do not mix together), and refrigerate until serving time, then toss at the table.

GLOSSARY OF GREENS AND LETTUCES

ARUGULA: Also called rugula and rocket, this sharp, peppery green has become very popular in the past few years. Usually sold in small bunches, its leaves can be sandy, so wash well. Toss with a strong vinaigrette and serve it solo or combine with subtler greens.

BELGIAN ENDIVE: This cigar-shaped, elegant green has small, cream-colored leaves that are tipped with yellow. It has a delicately bitter flavor and although it is fairly expensive, it is well worth the price.

BIBB LETTUCE: It has a small, tightly packed head. The leaves are pale in color with a delicate, "buttery" taste.

BOSTON LETTUCE: A small, loosely packed, and pale green head that is very tender and delicate in taste. Because the leaves are fragile, wash and dry with care.

CABBAGE: Green or red cabbages are commonly used in "slaws" or combined with other greens. Savoy cabbage is used in many salads because of its more delicate cabbage flavor. The food processor works best for finely shredding cabbage. I prefer using the medium slicing disk for shredding rather than the shredding disk.

CHICORY: Also called curly endive. Its blanched yellow center is surrounded by toothed dark green leaves. It is tart and crunchy and is best combined with milder leaves.

DANDELION GREENS: Tart in flavor, they are tasty in salads. You can forage for your own but commercially grown greens are more delicate in flavor.

ESCAROLE: A variety of endive with broad, curly leaves. It has a faintly tart flavor that mixes well with other greens.

ICEBERG LETTUCE: The common iceberg has gotten a lot of bad press lately because of its bland flavor. But its crisp and refreshing nature can be very agreeable when served well chilled with a creamy dressing.

LEAF LETTUCE: There are a number of varieties in this category. The most common are red and green leaf and oakleaf lettuce. Their frilly leaves never really form heads and they are crisp, yet tender with a lovely delicate taste.

MÂCHE: Also called lamb's lettuce and corn salad, this mild-flavored green is sold in small bunches. It is excellent either by itself or combined with other greens.

ROMAINE: The staple for the classic Caesar salad. It has crisp, long leaves with a distinctive taste that also contrasts pleasantly with other greens.

RADICCHIO: It looks like a tiny red cabbage. Its dramatic color and slightly bitter flavor combine well with other salad greens.

SPINACH: We all know that spinach is "good for us." It has a fine flavor and can be used alone or with other greens. Wash the leaves carefully to rid them of sand.

SORREL: This has a lemon-tart taste; its long, arrow-shaped leaves are wonderful mixed with milder salad greens. Young small leaves are best.

WATERCRESS: This refreshing, peppery green contrasts nicely with other greens or fruits such as oranges. It is also nice on its own.

TYPES OF OILS

OLIVE OIL: The peerless oil for most salad dressings. Its aroma and flavor range from light and fruity to unpleasantly harsh. I have tasted many expensive olive oils and not all are worth their high prices. Taste different brands until you find one you like. I prefer light and slightly spicy French olive oil and Italian olive oil with their more pronounced olive taste. *Extra-Virgin Olive Oil* is made from the very first pressing of the olives. It has an intense green-olive flavor and aroma, depending on the type of filtration system used. I personally find it too overpowering in most dressings, but many cooks prefer it. *Virgin Olive Oil* is my choice because it is lighter and sweeter in taste. Made from the second pressing, but still produced from the olive fruit, it is less expensive than extra-virgin. *Pure Olive Oil* is too bland and oily-flavored for salad dressings. It is manufactured by treating the previously pressed olive pulp with solvents. Refrigerate olive oil if not used frequently.

ALMOND, HAZELNUT, AND WALNUT OILS: Use alone or mix nut oils with light oils to add fragrance to salad dressings. Their nutty taste is sweet and delicate, but a little goes a long way. Since they quickly go rancid once opened, it is best to buy them in small quantities and store in the refrigerator.

PEPPER OILS: Flavored oils processed from grapeseed and spiced with peppercorns add a fillip of flavor to dressings. Refrigerate after opening.

HERB-FLAVORED OILS: These oils, made from either grapeseed or olive oil, are made with herbs and spices such as basil, bay leaf, tarragon, rosemary, garlic cloves, and peppercorns. Refrigerate after opening.

PEANUT OIL: This adds a sweetness to salads and is often used in Oriental dressings. Store in a cool, dark cupboard.

SUNFLOWER AND SAFFLOWER OILS: Very light in taste, these oils can be used alone or mixed with olive oil to produce a lighter dressing. Store as you would peanut oil.

SESAME OIL: Its strong, nutty tang adds a unique taste to dressings and is essential for salads with Oriental overtones. The best brands are from Japan. Refrigerate after opening.

TYPES OF VINEGARS

WINE VINEGAR: This vinegar, either red or white, is the most commonly used acid in dressings. Other wine vinegars are made from sherry or champagne, and herbs are often added to these vinegars for additional flavor. I always purchase vinegars in glass bottles because plastic imparts an adverse flavor.

FRUIT VINEGARS: Very popular today, especially raspberry vinegar. Other fruit vinegars include blueberry, cherry, blackberry, and peach. Light and obviously fruity-tasting, they add a special touch to dressings destined for both green and fruit salads.

HERB VINEGARS: Herbs like basil, tarragon, garlic, chive flowers, mint, thyme, and rosemary or a combination of these, are added to flavor vinegars.

CIDER VINEGAR: Reputed to have many healthy properties and nutrients, it has a tart, crisp flavor.

BALSAMIC VINEGAR: Italian *aceto balsamico* (aromatic vinegar) is a slowly aged vinegar with incredible flavor. This reddish-brown vinegar has a mellow, sweet-sour taste because of its long aging in small barrels made from different woods — red oak, chestnut, mulberry, and juniper wood. As it ages, the vinegar goes through a progression of barrels made from these different woods, each one giving a hint of their woody flavor.

RICE VINEGAR: Chinese rice vinegar has a sharp, clean acidic taste. The Japanese version is very mellow and sweet. They are excellent in any dressing and complement Oriental dressings made with sesame oil.

INGREDIENTS

ANCHOVIES: My recipes use the canned anchovy fillets in oil.

ARTICHOKE HEARTS: Not to be confused with marinated artichoke hearts, they are available canned in most specialty food shops.

AVOCADO: This buttery fruit should be eaten when the fruit yields to gentle pressure. If it is not quite ripe enough when you purchase it, leave at room temperature for a few days to ripen. Brush cut areas with lemon juice to prevent darkening. The finest varieties are the purplish-black and knobbly Haas, and the smooth, pear-shaped Fuerte.

BABY CORN: Also labeled Young Corn, these come in cans and are used mainly in Chinese stir-fries. Available in Chinese grocers, specialty shops, and many supermarkets in the Chinese food section.

BLACK OLIVES: I use Kalamata olives from Greece in my recipes. You may also use Niçoise olives from France. They are available in specialty food shops and in many supermarket delis. Canned American olives do not have the flavor or pungency needed for the recipes in this book.

BLACK PEPPER: I always use freshly ground black peppercorns. When I suggest "lots of freshly ground black pepper," I mean at least 20 grindings of the pepper mill.

CAPERS: These are the unopened flower buds of a Mediterranean shrub. Many cooks prefer the tiny French capers but I use the large variety in my salads because they have a stronger flavor. They are packed in vinegar (not salt), and I never rinse them.

CELERIAC: Also called celery root or knob celery. This type of celery is grown for its tasty, round knobby root. It has a delicate celery flavor and is traditionally sliced into matchstick-size pieces and tossed with Rémoulade dressing. Choose small, firm knobs, not more than 1 to 1½ pounds because they are more tender than the larger ones.

CHICKPEAS AND OTHER BEANS: Beans add their earthy taste and texture to many salads. White kidney beans (cannellini), red kidney beans, chickpeas, and lentils are available dried or precooked and canned. Although cooking your own dried beans is preferable for flavor and texture, in some recipes you can get away with using the canned variety.

CHILI PASTE WITH SOY BEAN: This hot and spicy condiment is widely used in China and adds a fiery taste and red tint to sauces. It is available in Oriental food stores.

DRIED HERBS: The fresher the dried herbs, the more flavorful your salads and dressings. Bottled herbs that have lost their color and aroma should be replaced.

FLOWERS: An attractive and colorful garnish for salads. Use individual petals or the whole flower, depending on the size. Use only flowers that have been grown without pesticides and be absolutely sure that the flowers you use are edible and won't cause you an allergic reaction. A few that are edible are: borage, chrysanthemum, day lily, geranium, lavender, nasturtium, pansies, roses, and violets.

FRESH HERBS: Do not substitute dried herbs if fresh are called for in a recipe. *Basil's* wonderful, pungent flavor complements almost every vegetable, especially tomatoes. Combine with other herbs except dill (with which it clashes) and use with assertive salad greens. *Borage* tastes faintly like cucumber and its refreshing flavor complements fish, shellfish, and most vegetable salads. *Chervil* is a parsley-like plant with a delicate aniselike flavor and feathery foliage. *Chives*, the mildest of the onion family, are useful for both their stems and their flowers. It is best to cut them with sharp scissors to prevent bruising. *Coriander* is a pungent herb also known as cilantro or Chinese parsley. *Dill* or dillweed blends particularly well with fish, shellfish, cucumber, and potatoes. *Mint* is a favorite in the Middle East. It is excellent with cucumbers, grains, and fruit-based salads and also blends well with yogurt dressings. *Parsley,* the most familiar fresh herb, blends well with most salad ingredients, especially when garlic abounds. There are two varieties: the common curly parsley and Italian parsley, a flat-leaf type that is preferred by many cooks. *Rosemary* has a wonderful piny aroma and slightly minty flavor.

It has an affinity to salads containing oranges. *Tarragon* is an aromatic herb that gives excellent flavor to salads containing greens, raw vegetables, and poultry. *Thyme* enhances many dressings with its delightful fragrance.

GARLIC: It is hard to imagine anyone not using garlic (lots of it!). If you're not passionate about a lot of garlic and would prefer a delicate hint of it, rub the inside of a salad bowl with a cut garlic clove before tossing your greens in it. Choose large bulbs that are tightly closed and not sprouting. Squeeze the bulb to make sure it is firm and fresh. Avoid powdered garlic.

GORGONZOLA: A very creamy, mold-ripened cheese from the Lombardy region of Italy. Its sharp flavor is wonderful in salads and salad dressings. It is available in Italian food shops or well-stocked cheese stores.

GRAINS: Excellent salads are made with grains such as cracked wheat and couscous. Besides their interesting texture and taste, they provide many nutrients as well as fiber.

HEARTS OF PALM: This delicate and fairly expensive vegetable is actually the interior of a small palm tree. The hearts look like white asparagus and have a lovely delicate flavor that complements many vegetable salads. They are available canned in specialty food shops.

JICAMA: A tropical root vegetable much appreciated by Mexicans, it tastes like a cross between a snow pea and a potato.

MUSTARDS: Mustards vary considerably in strength, flavor, and consistency. *Grainy Mustards* are coarse in texture and very aromatic. *Dijon and Dijon-style Mustard* is the most versatile mustard because of its smooth texture and well-rounded flavor. It is made from husked and ground mustard seeds, white wine vinegar, and spices.

NUTS AND SEEDS: These add interesting tastes and textures to salads. Both are enhanced by lightly toasting before use. My favorites are almonds, pecans, hazelnuts, pine nuts (pignoli), and sesame, pumpkin, and sunflower seeds.

OKRA: This tropical plant native to Africa is either loved or detested because of its slippery texture. It is usually cooked but is also delicious raw in salads.

PARMESAN: Be sure to purchase Parmesan that has the words "Parmigiano Reggiano" or, second best, "Grana Padano" stamped on the rind. Always grate it fresh just before using because it begins to lose flavor after grating. It is available in Italian food shops or well-stocked cheese stores.

RED ONION: Use the delicate-flavored red onion in salads rather than the stronger cooking onion. The medium slicing disk of the food processor works best for slicing it paper-thin.

RICE: *Wild rice*, which is not actually a rice, but the seed of a water grass, adds a nice texture to salads because of its chewy texture. *Basmati rice* is an aromatic, flavorful rice from India. Substitute regular *long-grain rice* if basmati is not available.

SHALLOTS: These are delicately onion- and garlic-flavored. If they're unavailable, I often substitute a little minced garlic and onion.

SPROUTS: For a nice nippy or crunchy texture in your salads, add peppery radish sprouts, wispy alfalfa sprouts, or crunchy bean sprouts.

SQUID: To clean, gently pull head and body apart. Cut off the tentacles just in front of the eyes. Squeeze out the beak, located where the tentacles come together (it looks like a small white marble), and discard. Under cold running water, remove all the entrails inside the body sac. Peel off the purple membrane covering the body. Set aside tentacles and cleaned body sac and continue until all the squid are cleaned. Rinse tentacles and follow recipe instructions.

SUN-DRIED TOMATOES: These have become very popular in North America in the past few years. Pumate San Remo from Liguria, Italy, is considered the best brand. They are available in most specialty and Italian food shops.

TOMATOES Use only flavorful, ripe, unwaxed tomatoes. If they're not fully ripe when you purchase them, do not refrigerate; instead, allow them to ripen at room temperature. There is no need to skin or seed tomatoes unless specified.

ZEST: The colored outer layer of skin on a citrus fruit.

EQUIPMENT

BOWLS: Large noncorrosive bowls — the larger the better — for tossing salads. I toss my salads in an extra-large stainless steel bowl that is around 13 inches or 16 inches in diameter, depending on the amount of greens; then I transfer ingredients to a more attractive salad bowl. I prefer glass or white salad bowls to accentuate and not compete with the color of the ingredients. I am not partial to wooden salad bowls because they become musty with age.

CHEESE GRATER: For grating Parmesan or other hard cheeses. I also use the four-sided cheese grater for finely grated zest (the smallest openings) and for grated zest (the largest openings).

FOOD PROCESSOR: Excellent for grating hard cheeses and combining many dressings, especially mayonnaise, also for slicing onions and shredding cabbage for slaws.

PEPPER MILL: Essential for salad-making and for the table.

RUBBER SPATULA: A spatula is handy for scraping out the salad ingredients from the "tossing" bowl into the salad bowl.

SALAD SERVERS: Useful implements for tossing salads, or use your hands to gently toss greens.

SALAD SPINNER: This gadget works exceptionally well for drying washed greens and lettuces.

WIRE WHISK: A small whisk is useful for mixing salad dressings.

♦ ♦ ♦

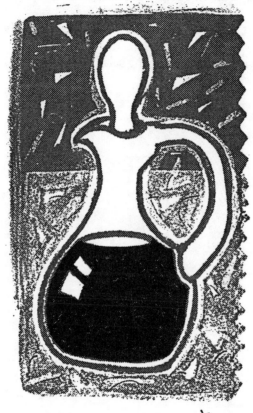

cruet

SALAD DRESSINGS

◆ ◆ ◆

Make this all-purpose, do-ahead
vinaigrette early in the day.
♦ For more piquancy, add several
thinly sliced white onions and
allow to marinate, then tumble with Boston
lettuce or a variety of mixed greens.

BASIC VINAIGRETTE

2 large garlic cloves, minced | 1 tablespoon dry mustard
1/2 teaspoon salt | 3 tablespoon tarragon vinegar
Lots of freshly ground black | 1/2 cup vegetable oil
  pepper

WHISK GARLIC, salt, pepper, dry mustard, and vinegar in a
small bowl until well combined. Drizzle in oil in a thin stream,
whisking until blended. Makes about 1/2 cup.

B

e sure to try this aromatic dressing. It adds a flourish to any salad greens. ◆ Top with croutons to make your salad even more scrumptious.

MINT AND CHIVE DRESSING

1 large garlic clove
1 teaspoon finely grated lime
   zest
2 tablespoons Dijon-style
   mustard
Salt

Freshly ground black
   pepper
¼ cup red wine vinegar
½ cup roughly chopped
   fresh mint
½ cup chopped fresh chives
¾ cup vegetable oil

CHOP GARLIC in a food processor. Add lime zest, mustard, salt, pepper, vinegar, mint, and chives and process to combine. With machine running, drizzle in oil until well blended. Makes about 1 cup.

Gorgeous fresh-garden flavor and pretty coral color. ◆ Drizzle over romaine lettuce and cherry tomatoes, or marinate blanched green beans or asparagus in this dressing.

TOMATO-DILL VINAIGRETTE

1 cup ripe cherry tomatoes
2 tablespoons canned tomato juice
2 large shallots
2 large garlic cloves
½ teaspoon salt
Lots of freshly ground black pepper

1 teaspoon finely grated lemon zest
2 tablespoons fresh lemon juice
1 tablespoon red wine vinegar
½ cup mild olive oil
1 tablespoon chopped fresh dill

PUREE CHERRY TOMATOES and tomato juice in a food processor. Rub the mixture through a strainer, pushing down with the back of a soup ladle, to remove skin and seeds. Set aside.

Rinse bowl of food processor to remove any seeds, then mince the shallots and garlic. With motor running add salt, pepper, lemon zest, lemon juice, vinegar, and oil until well blended. Pour into a container and stir in chopped dill. Makes about 1 cup.

ZESTY VINAIGRETTE

⅔ cup vegetable oil
5 tablespoons fresh lemon
juice
2 tablespoons red wine
vinegar
3 tablespoons finely diced
sweet red pepper

2 tablespoons minced green
onion (white part only)
1 tablespoon minced garlic
2½ teaspoons sugar
2 teaspoons dried oregano
2 teaspoons dry mustard
½ teaspoon salt
Freshly ground black pepper

WHISK OIL, lemon juice, vinegar, red pepper, green onion, garlic, sugar, oregano, mustard, salt, and pepper until well combined. Let stand for 15 minutes to blend flavors before using. Whisk again before drizzling over salad. Makes about 1½ cups.

Next time you toss a salad, remember this one. ♦ I developed a similar version for a Crisco advertising campaign and because of its sprightly flavor and pretty flecks of red and green, it's become a personal favorite. ♦ Don't chop the ingredients in a food processor — they must be finely diced with a good sharp knife — or the dressing turns orange in color.

citrus juicer

This delicious, pale-green, creamy dressing is thick enough to use as a dip too! ♦ Very tasty over a taco salad — tortillas mounded with shredded crisp lettuce, shredded Cheddar or Monterey Jack cheese, and chopped tomatoes.

AVOCADO DRESSING

1 large garlic clove
1 small onion, quartered
2 small (about 14 ounces) ripe avocados, peeled
½ cup plain natural yogurt
¼ cup vegetable oil

4 tablespoons fresh lemon juice
1 teaspoon Tabasco
Salt
Freshly ground black pepper

CHOP GARLIC and onion in a food processor. Add avocados, yogurt, oil, lemon juice, Tabasco, salt, and pepper and process until smooth. Makes about 2 cups.

ndeniably delicious. ◆ Superb with delicate greens, or over cooked green and white cheese-filled tortellini or other pasta salads.

SUN-DRIED TOMATO DRESSING

8 large sun-dried tomatoes
   in oil, drained and finely
   diced
1 tablespoon Dijon-style
   mustard

4 tablespoons fresh lemon
   juice
Salt
Freshly ground black pepper
½ cup olive or vegetable oil

COMBINE SUN-DRIED TOMATOES, mustard, lemon juice, salt, and pepper in a small bowl. Drizzle in oil, whisking to blend. Makes about ⅔ cup.

This dressing adds an oriental touch to marinated vegetables, or compose a salad of cooked shrimp, chopped cucumber, green onion, radishes, and fresh coriander leaves, then spoon onto a nest of bean sprouts. ♦ Drizzle dressing over top and sprinkle with toasted sesame seeds.

SESAME DRESSING

½ cup vegetable oil
¼ cup rice wine vinegar
2 tablespoons sesame oil
2 tablespoons soy sauce

1 large egg yolk
1 teaspoon dry mustard
1 teaspoon sugar
¼ teaspoon cayenne

COMBINE OIL, vinegar, sesame oil, soy sauce, egg yolk, dry mustard, sugar, and cayenne in a food processor until thickened. Makes about 1 cup.

veryone loves this delectable dressing. ◆ It's delicious on delicate greens, citrus, and avocado salads.

ORANGE TARRAGON DRESSING

1 large garlic clove
1 large shallot
Finely grated zest of
  2 medium oranges
¼ cup fresh orange juice
3 tablespoons red wine
  vinegar

2 tablespoons whole grain
  mustard
2 teaspoons dried tarragon
Salt
Freshly ground black pepper
¾ cup vegetable oil

MINCE GARLIC and shallot in a food processor. Add orange zest, orange juice, vinegar, mustard, tarragon, salt, and pepper and process to combine. With motor running, drizzle in oil in a thin stream until blended. Makes about 1 cup.

Sweet and zesty. ◆ I like this dressing over a mixture of greens such as red oakleaf, Boston lettuce, baby curly endive, and chunks of cantaloupe, or try it drizzled over watercress and fresh mandarin orange sections, or your own favorite citrus salad.

HONEY ORANGE POPPY SEED DRESSING

²/₃ cup vegetable oil
¹/₄ cup fresh lime juice
Grated zest of 1 medium
  orange
3 tablespoons fresh orange
  juice
3 tablespoons liquid honey

6 tablespoons finely diced
  red onion
1 tablespoon poppy seeds
1 teaspoon celery seeds
¹/₄ teaspoon dry mustard
Salt
Freshly ground black pepper

WHISK OIL, lime juice, orange zest, orange juice, honey, onion, poppy seeds, celery seeds, dry mustard, salt, and pepper until thoroughly blended. Let stand for 30 minutes to allow flavors to blend. Use immediately or cover and refrigerate until ready to use. Whisk again before using. Makes about 1 ¹/₃ cups.

BASIC MAYONNAISE

2 large egg yolks
1 to 2 tablespoons Dijon-
  style mustard, or to taste
½ teaspoon salt
⅛ teaspoon cayenne
Freshly ground black
  pepper

2 tablespoons fresh lemon
  juice, or to taste
1 to 1½ cups best-quality
  olive oil
Heavy or whipping cream
  for thinning sauce if
  necessary

PUT EGG YOLKS, mustard, salt, cayenne, pepper, and lemon juice in a food processor (or bowl). Process to mix ingredients and with motor running (or whisking constantly) add oil in a thin (at first drop by drop) stream until thickened. Thin with a little cream if necessary. Refrigerate if not using immediately. Makes about 1¼ to 1¾ cups.

Variations:
Tarragon Mayonnaise: add 1 teaspoon dried tarragon to basic recipe.
Lemon Mayonnaise: follow directions for basic mayonnaise, adding 2 to 3 teaspoons grated lemon zest.
Tangerine Mayonnaise: follow directions for basic mayonnaise, omitting lemon juice, adding 1 small garlic clove, minced, 2 teaspoons grated tangerine zest, and 1 tablespoon thawed frozen tangerine juice concentrate.
Lime Mayonnaise: follow directions for basic mayonnaise, omitting lemon juice, adding lime juice and 2 to 3 teaspoons grated lime zest.
Green Mayonnaise: follow directions for basic mayonnaise, adding at least 3 tablespoons fresh minced chives, parsley, or watercress leaves.
Other variations: add minced garlic to taste; shallots; herbs; flavored vinegars in place of lemon juice; and flavored mustards.

*M*ayonnaise can be made by hand with a whisk (tough on the wrist!) or very easily in a food processor or blender. ♦ If the mayonnaise curdles while adding the oil, beat another egg yolk in a clean bowl or food processor and gradually beat the curdled mayonnaise into the egg yolk until smooth, then proceed with recipe.

C*lassic American and superb
on romaine lettuce and also
fish or seafood salads.*

GREEN GODDESS DRESSING

1 cup mayonnaise
4 anchovy fillets, minced
1 tablespoon dried tarragon
¼ cup finely chopped fresh
   parsley
¼ cup finely chopped green
   onions (green part only)

1 tablespoon fresh lemon
   juice
Salt
Freshly ground black
   pepper

COMBINE MAYONNAISE, anchovies, tarragon, parsley, green onions, lemon juice, salt, and pepper in a bowl and refrigerate a few hours before using. Makes about 1½ cups.

B

eautiful with seafood — try it with a combination of cooked shrimp mounded on a nest of shredded greens and sliced cherry tomatoes, topped with dressing, then sprinkled with croutons. ♦ It's equally tantalizing with crisp greens.

THOUSAND ISLAND DRESSING

1 cup mayonnaise
1/4 cup finely chopped sweet
  red pepper
2 tablespoons bottled chili
  sauce
2 green onions, chopped

1 tablespoon chopped fresh
  parsley
1/4 teaspoon salt
1/4 teaspoon freshly ground
  black pepper

BLEND MAYONNAISE, red pepper, chili sauce, green onion, parsley, salt, and pepper in a bowl (or chop and blend ingredients in a food processor) until well combined. Chill before serving. Makes 1 1/4 cups.

Especially creamy, cool, and refreshing. ◆ This dressing complements any combination of crisp greens such as curly endive, radicchio, romaine, and Boston lettuce.

CREAMY CUCUMBER DRESSING

1 large garlic clove	1/2 cup sour cream
3 tablespoons roughly chopped fresh dill	1/2 cup plus 2 tablespoons mayonnaise
1 cup peeled and sliced English cucumber	Salt
	Freshly ground black pepper

CHOP GARLIC, dill, and cucumber in a food processor. Add sour cream, mayonnaise, salt, and pepper and process until smooth. Chill before serving. Makes about 2 cups.

THE ULTIMATE BLUE CHEESE DRESSING

1 large garlic clove
2 heaping tablespoons
   roughly chopped fresh dill
2/3 cup (about 3 ounces)
   crumbled blue cheese
1 cup sour cream
1/3 cup mayonnaise

2 tablespoons vegetable oil
2 tablespoons red wine
   vinegar
1 teaspoon Worcestershire
   sauce
1/4 teaspoon Tabasco

CHOP GARLIC and dill in a food processor. Add 1/2 cup blue cheese, sour cream, mayonnaise, oil, vinegar, Worcestershire sauce, and Tabasco. Process until smooth. Transfer to a bowl and stir in remaining crumbled blue cheese. Chill before serving. Makes about 1 3/4 cups.

D*elicious with watercress, crisp salad greens, tomato wedges, and red onion slices. ◆ The amount of blue cheese can be varied depending on how sharply flavored or pungent the blue-veined cheese is.*

L ovely, zesty flavor similar to Caesar Salad Dressing but much less pungent. ♦ Toss over steamed green beans, asparagus, or a simple salad of romaine lettuce and ripe summer tomatoes. ♦ Some minced fresh herbs may be added to taste.

mustard

CREAMY PARMESAN DRESSING

1 large garlic clove
1 egg yolk
1 tablespoon Dijon-style mustard
¼ cup freshly grated Parmesan cheese
2 tablespoons red wine vinegar

1 tablespoon fresh lemon juice
¼ teaspoon dried oregano
Salt
Freshly ground black pepper
½ cup mild olive or vegetable oil

CHOP GARLIC in a food processor. Add egg yolk, mustard, Parmesan cheese, vinegar, lemon juice, oregano, salt, and pepper and process until combined. With motor running, drizzle in oil until well blended. Makes about 1 cup.

think this robust vinaigrette enlivens any salad. ◆ It's very, very garlicky, so be warned.

CREAMY GARLIC DRESSING

2 large garlic cloves
1 egg yolk
3 tablespoons red wine
   vinegar
2 tablespoons Dijon-style
   mustard

½ cup fresh parsley
Salt
Freshly ground black
   pepper
½ cup vegetable oil

CHOP GARLIC in a food processor. Add egg yolk, vinegar, mustard, parsley, salt, and pepper and process to combine. With motor running, drizzle in oil until well blended. Makes about 1 cup.

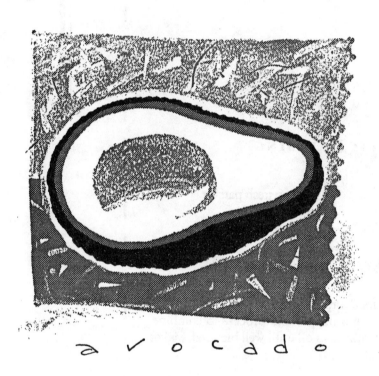

a v o c a d o

VEGETABLE

SALADS

◆ ◆ ◆

I t is essential to use young, tender dandelion leaves, as the older ones are tough and somewhat bitter. ◆ The chopped fresh mint complements the dandelion greens and the warm bacon dressing helps to counteract any acidity.

DANDELION AND MINT SALAD WITH WARM BACON DRESSING

1 large bunch dandelion greens, tough stalks removed
⅓ cup finely chopped fresh parsley
⅓ cup chopped fresh mint leaves
8 slices bacon

3 large garlic cloves, finely chopped
2 tablespoons red wine vinegar
2 teaspoons sugar
Salt
Freshly ground black pepper

PLACE DANDELION LEAVES in a large noncorrosive bowl. Add parsley and mint, then toss with hands to mix leaves. Set aside.

Cook bacon until crisp, remove to a paper-towel-lined plate, then crumble. Add garlic to bacon drippings and cook until soft but not brown.

Combine vinegar, sugar, salt, and pepper in a small bowl and add to drippings. Stir to dissolve salt and sugar, then pour over greens. Toss to coat evenly and top with crumbled bacon. Serves 4.

SUMMER SALAD WITH NASTURTIUMS

1 head red leaf lettuce
1 head bibb lettuce
1 bunch arugula, large
   stems removed
1 bunch watercress, large
   stems removed
4 tablespoons chopped
   fresh chives
¼ cup chopped fresh
   parsley
3 tablespoons chopped
   fresh tarragon

10 nasturtium flowers plus
   several small leaves
⅔ cup best-quality olive oil
3 to 4 tablespoons fresh
   lemon juice
2 teaspoons Dijon-style
   mustard
1 small garlic clove, minced
Salt
Freshly ground black
   pepper

TEAR LETTUCES and greens into manageable pieces and place with herbs (not nasturtiums) in a large salad bowl. Toss with hands to mix leaves.

Whisk oil, lemon juice, mustard, garlic, salt, and pepper in a small bowl and drizzle on enough vinaigrette to lightly coat the greens. Toss gently and sprinkle nasturtium flowers and leaves over top of salad just before serving, so that they do not become stained by the dressing. Serves 6.

*G*arden-fresh greens (the younger the better), herbs, and refreshingly spicy nasturtiums make this a very fragrant salad.

C*ool and refreshing, this salad must be served well chilled. It goes particularly well with fried and barbecued foods.* ♦ *My mother feels that a little sugar is needed; taste, and add if you agree.* ♦ *Use the slicing disk of a food processor for slicing cucumber and onion.*

CUCUMBER SOUR CREAM SALAD

1 large English cucumber, peeled and thinly sliced
1 medium red onion, thinly sliced
2 cups sour cream

3 tablespoons white wine vinegar, or to taste
Salt
Lots of freshly ground black pepper
Sugar (optional)

COMBINE CUCUMBER, onion, sour cream, vinegar, salt, and pepper in a large bowl and refrigerate several hours before serving. Taste and adjust seasoning if necessary. Serves 4.

CAESAR SALAD

2 to 3 medium garlic cloves
6 to 8 anchovy fillets,
   drained
1 tablespoon Dijon-style
   mustard
Salt
Freshly ground black
   pepper
½ cup best-quality olive oil

4 to 5 tablespoons fresh
   lemon juice
1 small egg
1 large head romaine lettuce
½ to ⅔ cup freshly grated
   Parmesan cheese
Croutons (recipe follows)*

MINCE GARLIC in a food processor. Add anchovies and mince. Add mustard, salt, and pepper and combine.

With the motor running, add oil in a thin stream until thickened. Add lemon juice and egg and turn on motor a few seconds to combine.

Tear lettuce leaves into manageable pieces and place in a very large salad bowl. Pour over dressing and toss. Sprinkle over Parmesan cheese, toss again, and top with croutons.

Serve at once and pass the pepper mill for each person to add to taste. Serves 6.

*To Make Croutons: Melt 1 tablespoon butter with 5 tablespoons best-quality olive oil in a large skillet. Add 2 small garlic cloves, minced; 1 teaspoon oregano; and ½ teaspoon thyme. Cut 5 slices day-old bread (crusts removed) into ½-inch cubes and fry until lightly browned. Remove to a paper-towel-lined plate to drain. This may be done several hours ahead.

*B*y now I'm sure everyone has heard the story of this classic salad, created by a restaurateur in Tijuana, Mexico, in the 1920s. ◆ I prefer my Caesar dressing to be pungent with anchovies and garlic and I also like to make it in a food processor to completely blend the raw egg.

A *very simple Italian dish that makes a wonderfully fragrant and savory salad, appetizer, or vegetable dish.*

ROASTED RED PEPPER SALAD

2 sweet red peppers	1 medium garlic clove,
2 sweet yellow peppers	minced
½ anchovy fillet	Salt
¼ cup-best quality olive oil	

ROAST PEPPERS under broiler (using broiler pan to catch moisture drippings) until charred and blistered. Set aside until cool enough to handle, then cut in half, remove peel and seeds. Cut into large strips, pat dry, and place in bowl.

Mash anchovy with a little of the oil in a small bowl, then add remaining oil, garlic, and a little salt. Pour over peppers, mix gently to coat evenly. Refrigerate several hours or overnight. Taste and adjust seasoning if necessary and serve at room temperature. Serves 2 to 4.

JICAMA AND ORANGE SALAD WITH CHILI DRESSING

1 small jicama, peeled and
    cut into julienne
4 medium navel oranges,
    peeled, pith removed,
    and separated into
    segments
1 small red onion, thinly
    sliced
¼ cup safflower oil

1 medium garlic clove,
    minced
1 to 2 tablespoons red wine
    vinegar
¼ teaspoon sugar
¼ teaspoon salt
½ teaspoon chili powder
Leaf lettuce, shredded

PLACE JICAMA, oranges, and onion in a salad bowl.
Whisk oil, garlic, vinegar, sugar, salt, and chili powder in a small bowl, then pour over ingredients. Toss gently and divide onto individual salad plates lined with shredded lettuce. Serves 6.

The combination of jicama and oranges bathed in a chili-powder-spiked dressing is marvelously refreshing and unusual.

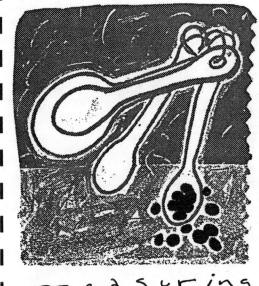

measuring spoons

Authentic Greek salad usually contains only tomatoes, onion, black olives, and feta cheese. When it does contain lettuce, it should be thinly sliced — not torn. ◆ This salad with its intriguing combination of sharp cheese, pungent olives, tomatoes, greens, and hint of mint is perfectly delicious.

GREEK SALAD WITH MINT DRESSING

½ large head romaine lettuce, thinly sliced
2 large ripe tomatoes, quartered
1 small red onion, thinly sliced
½ pound feta cheese, cubed
30 Greek olives (Kalamata), unpitted
⅓ cup best-quality olive oil

2 tablespoons red wine vinegar
1 small garlic clove, minced
Salt
Freshly ground black pepper
1 teaspoon dried oregano
1 tablespoon chopped fresh mint

PLACE LETTUCE, tomatoes, onion, feta cheese, and olives in a large salad bowl.

Whisk oil, vinegar, garlic, salt, and pepper in a small bowl, stir in oregano and mint, and pour over salad ingredients. Toss gently but thoroughly and serve at once. Serves 4.

CELERIAC WITH RÉMOULADE DRESSING

1 to 1½ pounds whole
  celeriac, peeled, cut into
  julienne, and tossed with
  a little lemon juice.
3 tablespoons Dijon-style
  mustard
⅓ cup safflower oil

⅓ cup best-quality olive oil
1 tablespoon tarragon
  vinegar
3 tablespoons heavy cream
2 teaspoons dried tarragon
Lettuce leaves

TOSS CELERIAC and lemon juice in a bowl and set aside.
  Put mustard in a food processor and, with motor running, gradually add oils in a very thin stream until thickened. Turn off machine, add 1 tablespoon each vinegar and cream, and combine. Add remaining cream a tablespoon at a time, combining between each addition. Add tarragon and combine.
  Toss celeriac with dressing, making sure it is completely coated. Chill for 2 hours and serve on a glass plate lined with lettuce leaves. (Radicchio leaves would be very dramatic.) Serves 4 to 6.

Raw celeriac (celery root) is dressed in a rich, tangy sauce. ◆ Celeriac darkens on exposure to air, so peel and toss with a little lemon juice right away.

Spectacular color and unusual flavor, this is not your ordinary beet salad.

BEET SALAD

4 medium beets with tops	½ teaspoon sugar
⅓ cup best-quality olive oil	Salt
5 tablespoons red wine vinegar, or to taste	Freshly ground black pepper
½ teaspoon dried thyme	2 green onions (green part only), finely chopped
¼ teaspoon mace	

LEAVE 1 INCH of beet stems and do not trim off taproots. Discard all but 10 of the smallest leaves from the beets. Bake beets in about an inch of water in a preheated 350°F oven until tender, about 30 to 60 minutes, depending on the age of the beets. Allow to cool only enough to handle; while still warm remove their skins. Cut into julienne and place in a medium bowl.

Whisk oil, vinegar, thyme, mace, sugar, salt, and pepper in a small bowl until thickened. Pour over beets, toss, and refrigerate for a few hours.

Just before serving, taste for seasoning, and add green onions. Shred beet tops, add to beets, and toss again. Serves 4 to 6.

HEARTS OF PALM, BABY CORN, ARTICHOKE, AND RADICCHIO SALAD

14-ounce (398-mL) can hearts of palm, drained and sliced

14-ounce (398-mL) can whole baby corn, drained and sliced lengthwise into quarters

14-ounce (398-mL) can artichoke hearts, drained and sliced in half

20 Greek olives (Kalamata), unpitted

½ pound mushrooms, wiped clean and sliced

1 large head radicchio, thinly sliced

½ head romaine lettuce, thinly sliced

½ cup best-quality olive oil

2 tablespoons tarragon vinegar

1 tablespoon Dijon-style mustard

½ teaspoon sugar

Salt

Lots of freshly ground black pepper

3 tablespoons dried tarragon

COMBINE HEARTS OF PALM, baby corn, artichoke hearts, olives, mushrooms, radicchio, and romaine in a large salad bowl.

Whisk oil, vinegar, mustard, sugar, salt, pepper, and tarragon in a small bowl and pour over vegetables. Toss gently and serve. Serves 10.

ull of lovely, crunchy vegetables, this salad can feed a large crowd. ◆ The following recipe is only a suggestion; feel free to improvise with ingredients you have on hand.

mushrooms

A *happy marriage of fresh garden greens in a tart dressing.*

POTPOURRI SALAD WITH LIME SORREL DRESSING

4 quarts lightly packed
  mixed greens (equal
  amounts of torn endive,
  oakleaf, bibb, and sorrel)
⅔ cup best-quality olive oil
2 to 3 tablespoons fresh
  lime juice

2 tablespoons chopped
  fresh sorrel
2 tablespoons finely
  chopped fresh chives
Salt
Freshly ground black
  pepper

PLACE GREENS in a large salad bowl and toss with hands to mix leaves.

Combine oil, lime juice, sorrel, chives, salt, and pepper in a small bowl and drizzle on enough vinaigrette to lightly coat the greens. Toss gently and serve. Serves 10.

COBB SALAD

½ medium head iceberg lettuce, shredded
1 cup safflower or best-quality olive oil
¼ cup white wine vinegar, or to taste
1 tablespoon Dijon-style mustard
½ teaspoon salt
Lots of freshly ground black pepper
1 teaspoon dried tarragon
1 medium garlic clove, minced
8 large slices bacon, cooked until crisp, drained, and crumbled

1 large ripe avocado, pitted, peeled, cubed, and tossed with a little lemon juice
2 medium ripe tomatoes, seeded and cubed
1½ cups cubed cooked chicken (about 1 large whole chicken breast)
4 hard-cooked eggs, finely chopped
6 ounces blue cheese, preferably Roquefort, crumbled
1 small bunch watercress, large stems removed (garnish)

ARRANGE ICEBERG lettuce over bottom of a wide salad bowl.

Whisk oil, vinegar, mustard, salt, pepper, tarragon, and garlic in a small bowl. Drizzle a little vinaigrette over lettuce.

Arrange the bacon, avocado, tomatoes, chicken, and eggs in wedge-shaped rows over the lettuce. Place the blue cheese in the center. You may assemble the salad and refrigerate for up to an hour before serving.

To serve, drizzle salad with just enough vinaigrette to lightly coat. Gently toss ingredients to combine, garnish with watercress, and serve. Serves 6 to 8.

H*ooray for Hollywood!* ◆ *This salad was invented in the '30s by Robert Cobb, proprietor of Hollywood's Brown Derby Restaurant. It stars chicken, crisp bacon, tomatoes, eggs, avocado, and Roquefort cheese.*

Don't say I didn't warn you!
♦ There is nothing subtle
about this cole slaw, which
is ultimate bliss for garlic
lovers. ♦ It is wonderful with basic
barbecues and seafood feasts. ♦ Use the
medium slicing disk (not the shredding
disk) of a food processor for shredding
cabbage.

GARLICKY COLE SLAW

1 medium green cabbage,
  trimmed, cored, and
  shredded
4 to 6 large garlic cloves,
  minced

2 cups mayonnaise
½ cup sugar
1 teaspoon salt
¼ cup cider vinegar

TOSS CABBAGE and garlic in a large noncorrosive bowl (hands work best) until garlic is evenly distributed. Add mayonnaise and stir to mix.

In a separate bowl, stir sugar, salt, and vinegar and pour over cabbage. Mix well and refrigerate several hours or overnight before serving. When serving, drain away excess liquid. Serves 8.

CREAMY COLE SLAW

1 pound cabbage, trimmed, cored, and shredded	2 tablespoons red wine vinegar
2 medium carrots, shredded	2 teaspoons sugar
1 medium sweet red pepper, seeded and shredded	Salt
	Freshly ground black pepper
1 small green pepper, seeded and shredded	1 cup mayonnaise
1 small red onion, finely chopped	2 tablespoons heavy cream
	2 teaspoons caraway seeds

COMBINE CABBAGE, carrots, red and green peppers, and onion in a very large bowl.

Combine vinegar, sugar, salt, pepper, mayonnaise, cream, and caraway seeds in another bowl and add to vegetables. Stir well to mix, cover, and refrigerate several hours before serving. Stir again before serving and drain if necessary. Serves 4 to 6.

T*he harmonious contrasts of colors and textures make a pretty and vivid-tasting cole slaw.* ◆ *The medium slicing disk (not the shredding disk) of a food processor works best for shredding the vegetables, except the carrots, for which you should use the shredding disk.*

c a b b a g e

Red-purple cabbage makes one of the most beautiful salads. ◆ It is simple to make and is striking on a buffet table. ◆ Use the medium slicing disk (not the shredding disk) of a food processor for shredding cabbage. ◆ Add the dried currants if you prefer a slightly sweet cole slaw.

RED CABBAGE SLAW

1 medium red cabbage, trimmed, cored, and shredded
1 small red onion, thinly sliced
1 cup shredded carrots
1 large sweet red pepper, thinly sliced

¾ cup dried currants (optional)
2 cups mayonnaise
3 tablespoons red wine vinegar
Salt

COMBINE CABBAGE, onion, carrots, red pepper, currants, mayonnaise, vinegar, and salt in a large (preferably glass) bowl and refrigerate several hours before serving. Serves 8 to 10.

P*opular in Southern cooking, okra is also delicious raw.*
♦ *It is best to serve this salad the instant the ingredients are cut up and tossed.*

Okra, Tomato, and Mushroom Salad

2 large ripe tomatoes, cut into 1-inch cubes
½ pound mushrooms, wiped clean and thinly sliced
¾ pound small, bright green okra, cut into ¼-inch slices

¼ cup roughly chopped fresh basil leaves
⅓ cup best-quality olive oil
1 to 1½ tablespoons red wine vinegar
Salt
Freshly ground black pepper

COMBINE TOMATOES, mushrooms, okra, and basil in a salad bowl.

Whisk oil, vinegar, salt, and pepper in a small bowl and pour over vegetables. Toss and serve at once. Serves 4 to 6.

onderful, homey potato salad. ◆ *Lovely for a picnic or a barbecue or as an additional offering on the buffet table.*

OLD-FASHIONED POTATO SALAD

9 to 10 medium potatoes
½ cup potato water
3 tablespoons vinegar
Salt
Lots of freshly ground black pepper
1 small red onion, finely chopped
1 medium rib celery, finely chopped
3 hard-cooked eggs, finely chopped
½ cup finely chopped fresh parsley
¾ cup mayonnaise

SCRUB UNPEELED POTATOES and boil until tender but not mushy (or too firm either). Drain, reserving ½ cup potato water. Allow potatoes to cool only enough to handle them, then peel. Cut into ½-inch cubes and place in a large bowl.

Combine vinegar and potato water in a small bowl and pour over potatoes. Add salt and pepper. Stir well but gently.

Add onion, celery, eggs, and parsley and mix. Place bowl in freezer, about 3 to 5 minutes, or just long enough to chill ingredients quickly. Remove and add mayonnaise.

Stir and adjust seasoning if necessary, and refrigerate at least several hours or overnight before serving. Serves 6.

FOUR GREENS WITH GRILLED BRIE OR STILTON

2 ounces radicchio
4 ounces chicory
  (curly endive)
2 ounces mâche
4 ounces red oakleaf
  lettuce
4 slices (cut on the diagonal
  about 1-inch thick)
  French bread
Softened butter
Dijon-style mustard
6 ounces Brie cheese, thinly
  sliced, or crumbled
  Stilton cheese

⅓ cup walnut, hazelnut,
  or best-quality olive oil
2 tablespoons red wine
  vinegar
1 teaspoon Dijon-style
  mustard
Salt
Freshly ground black
  pepper

TEAR GREENS into manageable pieces and place in a salad bowl. Toss gently with hands to mix leaves.

Preheat broiler. If using Brie, spread slices with butter and a little mustard. Place a slice of Brie on each piece of bread. If using Stilton, omit butter and mustard and place a portion of crumbled cheese on bread slices. Place bread on a baking sheet and cook until cheese is melted and bubbly, approximately 2 to 3 minutes.

Meanwhile whisk oil, vinegar, mustard, salt, and pepper in a small bowl and pour over greens. Toss gently and divide among 4 salad plates.

Place 1 hot cheese crouton in the center of each salad and serve immediately. Serves 4.

The colorful blend of delicate and bitter greens topped with a cheese crouton is a visual delight and fun to eat while waiting for the main course.

Joyous flavors of eggplant and sweet-tasting peppers— an Italian classic that is served as part of an antipasto, a salad, or a vegetable dish.

INSALATA SICILIANA

1 pound unpeeled eggplant, cut into ½-inch slices
Salt
3 sweet red peppers
4 medium ripe tomatoes, halved and seeded

3 tablespoons best-quality olive oil, plus extra for spooning over eggplant
1 medium garlic clove, minced
Salt

PLACE EGGPLANT in a colander and sprinkle with about 2 tablespoons salt. Allow to drain for 40 minutes.

Roast red peppers under broiler (using broiler pan to catch moisture drippings) until skin is charred and blistered on all sides. Set aside to cool.

Squeeze out moisture from halved and seeded tomatoes (this is important or salad will be watery), cut into 1-inch cubes, and place in a bowl.

Rinse eggplant under running water, then dry very well in a clean dish towel. Place on broiling rack, spoon some oil over top, and broil 10 minutes on each side, or until browned.

Remove charred skin from peppers, remove seeds, slice into ¼-inch strips, and add to tomatoes in bowl.

Slice eggplant pieces in half lengthwise and add to bowl. Add 3 tablespoons oil, garlic, and salt, stir gently, cover, and refrigerate for several hours or overnight before serving.

Bring back to room temperature before serving. Serves 4 to 6.

WATERCRESS, PEAR, AND BLUE CHEESE SALAD

1 large bunch watercress, large stems removed

1 medium Belgian endive, thinly sliced lengthwise

2 very firm small pears, unpeeled, cored, and cut into thick julienne

¼ cup pecan pieces, lightly toasted*

½ cup crumbled blue cheese

½ cup walnut or best-quality olive oil

2 tablespoons fresh lemon juice

2 teaspoons Dijon-style mustard

1 medium shallot, finely chopped

Salt

Freshly ground black pepper

COMBINE WATERCRESS and endive in a salad bowl. Add pears, pecans, and blue cheese.

Whisk oil, lemon juice, mustard, shallot, salt, and pepper in a small bowl. Drizzle enough dressing over salad to lightly coat, toss, and serve immediately. Serves 4.

*NOTE: Place pecans in an unoiled, heavy skillet. Place on moderate heat and cook until lightly browned.

eppery watercress, sweet pears, and pungent blue cheese combine to make a lovely, elegant salad that is excellent served with grilled meats.

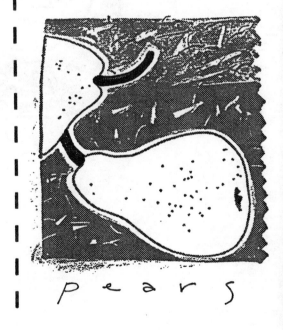

pears

Lemons

FRUIT
SALADS

◆ ◆ ◆

piquant, tart-tasting fruit salad that is meant to be served as a first course.

GRAPEFRUIT AND ORANGE SALAD WITH RASPBERRY VINAIGRETTE

1 pink grapefruit, peeled, pith removed, and sliced crosswise into ¼-inch rounds

1 large navel orange, peeled, pith removed, and sliced crosswise into ¼-inch rounds

4 tablespoons best-quality olive oil

1 to 2 tablespoons raspberry vinegar

1 small garlic clove, minced

¼ teaspoon dried oregano

Handful watercress, stems removed (garnish)

ALTERNATE GRAPEFRUIT and orange slices on 2 serving plates.

Whisk oil, vinegar, garlic, and oregano in a small bowl until slightly thickened. Drizzle over fruit and garnish with watercress leaves. Serves 2.

WALDORF SALAD WITH ORANGE ZEST AND SLIVERED ALMONDS

3 large McIntosh apples, unpeeled, cored, cut into cubes, and tossed with a little lemon juice
¼ cup dried currants
Grated zest of 2 large oranges
1 tablespoon fresh orange juice

1 medium rib celery, finely chopped
⅓ cup lightly toasted slivered almonds
½ cup mayonnaise
½ cup natural unflavored yogurt

COMBINE APPLES, currants, orange zest, orange juice, celery, almonds, mayonnaise, and yogurt in a noncorrosive bowl and refrigerate for several hours before serving. Serves 4.

est served the day it is prepared because the toasted almonds tend to overpower the dressing the longer it stands. ◆ *This classic American salad traditionally is made with walnuts, but I thought almonds would be a nice change of pace. By all means, use walnuts if you prefer.*

U nusual and delicious, this refreshing salad from Morocco is the perfect ending to a spicy meal.

MOROCCAN ORANGE AND DATE SALAD

2 medium navel oranges, peeled, pith removed, and separated into segments
12 pitted dates, sliced
3 tablespoons blanched slivered almonds
3 tablespoons fresh orange juice

2 tablespoons fresh lemon juice
1 tablespoon sugar
½ teaspoon powdered cinnamon
A few fresh mint leaves (optional garnish)

ARRANGE ORANGE segments in a single layer on a dinner plate or similar size serving dish. Sprinkle dates and almonds over oranges; cover with plastic wrap and chill.

Just before serving, mix juices and sugar in a small bowl until sugar dissolves. Spoon over salad and dust with cinnamon. Garnish with mint leaves, if desired, and serve. Serves 4.

ORANGE, RED ONION, AND AVOCADO SALAD

1 large navel orange peeled, pith removed, and thinly sliced
1 ripe avocado, peeled, pitted, and thinly sliced
1 small red onion, thinly sliced
10 Greek olives (Kalamata), unpitted
¼ cup best-quality olive oil
1 to 1½ tablespoons red wine vinegar
1 teaspoon Dijon-style mustard
Grated zest of 1 large orange
¼ cup fresh coriander leaves (garnish)

LINE A dinner plate (which acts as the serving platter) with the orange slices, then place the avocado slices in a spoke pattern on top of the oranges. Strew the onion slices over the orange-avocado slices. Strew on the olives.

Whisk oil, vinegar, mustard, and orange zest in a small bowl and spoon over salad. Garnish the center of the dish with coriander leaves. Serves 2.

onderful shades of orange, red, green, and black give this salad its dazzling appearance. And its wild and pungent flavors are guaranteed to wake up weary palates!

T

*his salad is a visual delight
— a colorful blend of green,
orange, red, and purple
flecked with black poppy
seeds.*

CANTALOUPE POMEGRANATE SALAD WITH HONEY POPPY SEED DRESSING

Radicchio leaves
1 honeydew melon, seeds
   removed, then pulp
   removed with a melon-
   ball cutter
1 cantaloupe, seeds removed,
   then pulp removed with a
   melon-ball cutter

½ small red onion, thinly
   sliced
½ large pomegranate, seeds
   removed carefully so
   they don't bruise
Honey Poppy Seed Dressing
   (see page 30)

LINE A glass serving dish with radicchio leaves, then arrange melons, onion, and pomegranate seeds attractively over lettuce.

Drizzle with enough Honey Poppy Seed Dressing to lightly coat and serve at once. Serves 4 to 6.

MEAT & POULTRY

SALADS

◆ ◆ ◆

Harry's Bar in Venice created Carpaccio — thinly sliced raw beef covered with slices of Parmesan and moistened with olive oil. ♦ This variation is served with a zesty mayonnaise and is wonderful as a first course or a light entrée.

CARPACCIO WITH ZESTY MAYONNAISE DRESSING

½ cup mayonnaise
6 anchovy fillets, roughly chopped
2 tablespoons capers, drained
¼ teaspoon hot red pepper flakes
¼ cup chopped fresh parsley
1 teaspoon Worcestershire sauce

1 to 2 teaspoons balsamic vinegar, or to taste
1 to 1½ pounds filet mignon*
Sprigs of fresh basil with large leaves (garnish)
8 Greek olives (Kalamata), unpitted (garnish)

MIX MAYONNAISE, anchovies, capers, red pepper flakes, parsley, Worcestershire sauce, and vinegar in a food processor until a coarse texture — do not overprocess into a paste. Transfer to a bowl and refrigerate a few hours before using.

Slice beef into paper-thin slices (you may freeze meat until firm enough to slice easily, about 45 minutes). Place about 5 overlapping slices of beef on each plate. Add a large dollop of dressing to each plate and garnish with a sprig of basil and 2 black olives. Serves 4.

*NOTE: Once the beef is sliced it must be served immediately or the beef will darken.

GRILLED CHICKEN SALAD WITH TROPICAL FRUITS

½ head leaf lettuce
1 bunch watercress, large stems removed
1 ripe papaya, peeled, pitted, and sliced
1 ripe mango, peeled, pitted, and sliced
1 medium navel orange, peeled, pith removed, and separated into segments

Grated zest of 2 limes
Juice of 2 limes
½ cup safflower oil
2 whole chicken breasts, boned but not skinned
Salt
Freshly ground black pepper

TEAR LETTUCE into manageable pieces and arrange on 4 salad plates. Place watercress leaves over lettuce and set aside.

Place papaya, mango, orange, lime zest, lime juice, and oil in a medium bowl, mix gently, and set aside for 20 minutes to marinate.

Sprinkle chicken with salt and pepper and grill on the underside for 3 minutes and the skin side for 6 to 10 minutes, or until cooked.

Arrange the fruit on top of the greens, leaving behind the marinade and retaining a nice border of green. Slice each cooked chicken breast with a very sharp knife across the grain and arrange on top of fruit. Spoon remaining marinade over chicken and serve. Serves 4.

The delicate grilled flavor of the chicken with mango, papaya, orange, and lime makes this a very appealing lunch or light dinner salad. ♦ Presentation is of utmost importance here.

L

ight and refreshing, this salad makes an engaging luncheon entrée, side dish, or a fine buffet dish.

CHICKEN OR TURKEY PASTA SALAD WITH APPLES, ORANGE ZEST, AND CURRANTS

½ pound medium pasta shells, cooked *al dente*, drained, and rinsed to cool with cold water

2 medium ribs celery, finely chopped

4 Granny Smith apples, unpeeled, cored, and chopped

½ cup dried currants

Grated zest of 2 large oranges

4 cups cooked chicken or turkey, skinned and torn into bite-size pieces

1 cup mayonnaise

¾ cup natural unflavored yogurt

Salt

Freshly ground black pepper

COMBINE PASTA, celery, apples, currants, orange zest, chicken or turkey, mayonnaise, yogurt, salt, and pepper in a non-corrosive bowl and refrigerate several hours before serving. Serves 6 to 8.

DUCK SALAD WITH
WARM SESAME DRESSING

1 small cucumber, peeled
  and thinly sliced
1 head red leaf lettuce,
  thinly sliced
¾ pound boned Chinese
  roast duck, skin removed
  and cut into julienne
2 tablespoons peanut oil
1 teaspoon finely chopped
  fresh ginger
1 medium garlic clove,
  finely chopped
¼ cup Oriental sesame oil

1 tablespoon red wine
  vinegar
1 tablespoon chili paste
  with soy bean
1 tablespoon sugar
Grated zest of 1 large orange
1 tablespoon sesame seeds,
  toasted
2 large green onions
  (green part only), finely
  chopped (garnish)
¼ cup roughly chopped
  fresh coriander (garnish)

ARRANGE CUCUMBER SLICES on outer edges of 4 salad plates. Place lettuce in the center of each plate and divide duck evenly among plates.

Heat peanut oil in a noncorrosive skillet and add ginger and garlic. Cook until ginger and garlic are tender, about 3 minutes. Add sesame oil, vinegar, chili paste, sugar, and orange zest and cook until heated. Drizzle over salads, sprinkle on sesame seeds, and garnish with green onions and coriander. Serves 4.

B*uy a half roast duck from a Chinese barbecue shop or restaurant and remove meat from bones.* ♦ *You can save the carcass for duck stock, if you wish.*

Ever-popular chicken salad. ♦ Here it is flavored with parsley, lemon, and Parmesan cheese. ♦ Broccoli, celery, and red pepper are added to make this a hearty, well-rounded salad.

CHICKEN SALAD WITH PARMESAN MAYONNAISE DRESSING

2 whole chicken breasts, cooked and skin removed
4 cups blanched broccoli flowerets
1 medium rib celery, cut into julienne
1 large sweet red pepper, seeded and cut into julienne
1 cup finely chopped fresh parsley

2 cups mayonnaise
1 to 2 tablespoons fresh lemon juice
¼ cup freshly grated Parmesan cheese, or to taste
Salt
Lots of freshly ground black pepper
Lettuce leaves

TEAR CHICKEN into bite-size pieces and mix with broccoli, celery, red pepper, parsley, mayonnaise, lemon juice, Parmesan cheese, salt, and pepper. Refrigerate several hours before serving. Serve on lettuce leaves. Serves 4 to 6.

TURKEY SALAD WITH CURRIED CHUTNEY DRESSING

3 cups cubed cooked turkey
½ small red onion, thinly sliced
1 large whole green onion, finely chopped
8-ounce (227-mL) can water chestnuts, rinsed under cold water, then sliced
¼ cup blanched slivered almonds
1 cup mayonnaise
½ cup natural unflavored yogurt
Grated zest of 1 large orange
1 tablespoon fresh orange juice
2 to 3 tablespoons mango chutney
4 teaspoons best-quality curry powder, or to taste
Salt
Freshly ground black pepper
Lettuce leaves
Grated zest of 1 medium orange (garnish)
Grated zest of 1 large lime (garnish)

PLACE TURKEY, onion, green onion, water chestnuts, and almonds in a salad bowl.

Combine mayonnaise, yogurt, orange zest, orange juice, chutney, curry powder, salt, and pepper in a small bowl and pour over turkey ingredients. Mix thoroughly but gently and refrigerate for several hours before serving.

Line a serving dish with lettuce, top with turkey salad, and garnish with orange and lime zest. Serves 4 to 6.

O f course you can substitute cooked chicken. ◆ Served on a bed of curly leaf lettuce and sprinkled with grated zest, or perhaps garnishes such as salted peanuts, shredded coconut, sliced bananas, and chopped apples, it makes a glamorous company dish.

Leaf Lettuce

FISH & SEAFOOD

SALADS

♦ ♦ ♦

This salad is thought to have originated in San Francisco. ♦ No one knows who "Louis" was, but he definitely inspired a glorious salad.

CRAB LOUIS

½ cup mayonnaise
½ cup sour cream
2 tablespoons ketchup
¼ teaspoon ground cloves
¼ teaspoon cayenne
2 teaspoons Dijon-style mustard
2 teaspoons drained prepared horseradish
1 teaspoon Worcestershire sauce
1 romaine lettuce heart, shredded
1 pound fresh or frozen crabmeat, drained and squeezed dry
Watercress (garnish)

COMBINE MAYONNAISE, sour cream, ketchup, cloves, cayenne, mustard, horseradish, and Worcestershire sauce in a medium bowl.

Divide shredded lettuce on 4 salad plates, mound crabmeat over it, top with sauce, and garnish with watercress. Serve promptly. Serves 4.

Spectacular and perfect to serve at a formal dinner or as an elegant first course. ◆ This recipe is easy to double or triple.

LOBSTER SALAD WITH LIME MAYONNAISE AND PINK PEPPERCORNS

2 cooked lobsters
 (1½ to 2 pounds each)
8 slices avocado
1 lime, thinly sliced

Lime mayonnaise
 (see page 31)
Grated zest of 1 large lime
Pink peppercorns (garnish)

REMOVE THE TAIL and claw meat from lobsters. Cut the tail in half lengthwise, then into chunks, and arrange chunks and 1 claw each on 4 glass salad plates. Place 2 slices of avocado and 3 lime slices decoratively beside lobster.

Dollop mayonnaise on top of lobster, sprinkle over lime zest, and sprinkle several peppercorns over top. Serves 4.

CALAMARI SALAD

1 pound cleaned squid, cut into ¼-inch rings; tentacles halved if large
2 tablespoons red wine vinegar
1 teaspoon salt
¾ cup best-quality olive oil
4 tablespoons balsamic or red wine vinegar
Grated zest of 1 large lemon
2 tablespoons fresh lemon juice
2 large garlic cloves, minced
Salt
Lots of freshly ground black pepper
2 teaspoons dried oregano
2 heaping tablespoons finely chopped fresh parsley
Romaine lettuce leaves

COOK THE SQUID in boiling water, vinegar, and salt until edges curl and squid pieces are opaque. If squid are small, it will take 30 to 60 seconds. Taste and continue cooking until tender, but do not overcook or they will be tough. Drain and cool.

Combine squid, oil, vinegar, lemon zest, lemon juice, garlic, salt, pepper, oregano, and parsley in a medium bowl and refrigerate for several hours or overnight before serving.

To serve, place a lettuce leaf on each plate and spoon squid with some of the marinade on top of lettuce. Serves 4.

M aybe it's because of its unfounded reputation as a monster in films and fiction that few Americans have tasted squid's delicate flavor. ♦ For whatever reason, once people try this delectable cephalopod properly cooked, they are no longer squeamish about eating squid. ♦ This is one of the nicest ways I know to prepare squid.

SALADE NICOISE

feast for the eye as well as the palate, this classic French salad is a wonderful meal in itself.

½ pound new potatoes, cooked until tender, cooled, and cut in half

¾ pound green beans, trimmed, cooked until crisply tender, and cooled

14-ounce (398-mL) can artichokes, drained and quartered

1 sweet yellow or red pepper, seeded and cut into julienne

3 to 4 medium ripe tomatoes, sliced into wedges

1 small red onion, thinly sliced

½ cup Niçoise or Kalamata olives, unpitted

⅓ cup chopped fresh parsley

6½-ounce (184-g) can chunk light or solid white (not flaked) tuna, drained

1 cup best-quality olive oil

1 tablespoon Dijon-style mustard

3 tablespoons red wine vinegar

2 medium garlic cloves, minced

½ teaspoon sugar

Salt

Lots of freshly ground black pepper

4 hard-cooked eggs, shelled and quartered

6 anchovy fillets

2 tablespoons capers

COMBINE POTATOES, green beans, artichokes, yellow or red pepper, tomatoes, onion, olives, and parsley in a large bowl. Break tuna into large pieces and add to ingredients.

Whisk oil, mustard, vinegar, garlic, sugar, salt, and pepper in a small bowl and pour half of vinaigrette over ingredients. Toss gently and transfer mixture to a large platter. Arrange egg wedges around edge of platter, decorate salad with anchovy fillets, and sprinkle on capers. Drizzle with enough vinaigrette to lightly coat and serve immediately. Serves 4 to 6.

RICE, BEANS, PASTA, & GRAIN

SALADS

◆ ◆ ◆

his is a refreshing Middle Eastern salad made with bulgur (cracked wheat), which is available in health food stores and specialty shops. ♦ *A great do-ahead dish that is excellent for buffets, or serve it as an hors d'oeuvre, using the inner leaves of romaine to scoop up the mixture.* ♦ *Do not use dried mint for this dish.*

TABBOULEH

1 cup bulgur wheat
1 large ripe tomato, chopped
2 large whole green onions, finely chopped (about ½ cup)
½ cup finely chopped fresh parsley
3 tablespoons chopped fresh mint leaves
¼ cup fresh lemon juice
¼ cup best-quality olive oil
Salt
Freshly ground black pepper
Inner leaves of romaine (garnish)
A few Kalamata olives, unpitted (garnish)

PUT BULGUR and 2 cups cold water in a large bowl and let stand for 30 minutes. Drain through a fine sieve, gently pushing out excess water.

Place bulgur in a glass bowl; add tomato, green onions, parsley, mint, lemon juice, oil, salt, and pepper and mix gently. Cover and refrigerate at least 2 hours. Taste and adjust seasoning if necessary, place romaine leaves around edge of bowl (standing up), and garnish with black olives. Serves 4 to 6.

RICE SALAD WITH TOMATOES, MUSHROOMS, AND TARRAGON

1½ cups long-grain rice
2 medium ripe tomatoes,
  cut into ½-inch cubes
½ pound mushrooms,
  wiped clean and thinly
  sliced
¼ cup finely chopped red
  onion

2 tablespoons dried
  tarragon
Freshly ground black
  pepper
½ cup vegetable oil
2 tablespoons red wine
  vinegar
Salt

COOK RICE in 3 cups water until water is absorbed and rice is tender, about 25 minutes. Remove to a salad bowl and cool to room temperature.

Add tomatoes, mushrooms, onion, tarragon, and pepper and combine.

Whisk oil, vinegar, and salt and pour over rice. Stir to combine and refrigerate for several hours before serving. Serves 6.

Rice lover that I am, this is one of my favorite side-dish salads.

N *othing could be better for a dinner party than this delectable rice salad chock-full of chicken, shrimp, smoked sausage, and vegetables.*

PAELLA SALAD

3 tablespoons best-quality olive oil
3 large garlic cloves, chopped
1 small onion, finely chopped
2 cups long-grain rice
4½ cups chicken broth
¼ teaspoon powdered saffron or 1 teaspoon saffron threads, crumbled
¼ teaspoon turmeric (or ½ teaspoon if not using saffron)
½ teaspoon dried thyme
⅔ cup best-quality olive oil
2 tablespoons red wine vinegar
¼ cup fresh lemon juice
1 large garlic clove, minced
¼ cup finely chopped fresh parsley
Salt
Lots of freshly ground black pepper

1 whole cooked chicken breast, skinned, boned, and cut into bite-size pieces
12 medium cooked shrimp, shelled and deveined
½ pound cooked chorizo or garlic-seasoned pork sausage, sliced
1 large sweet red pepper, seeded and diced
1 large ripe tomato, seeded and chopped
14-ounce (398-mL) can artichoke hearts, drained and sliced
1 cup fresh or frozen peas
6 large whole green onions, finely chopped
½ cup chopped fresh parsley
14 Greek olives (Kalamata), pitted and halved

HEAT OIL in a heavy, 4½-quart saucepan. Add garlic and onion and cook until tender, about 2 minutes. Add rice and stir to coat with oil. Add broth, saffron, turmeric, and thyme. Cover and bring to the boil. Reduce heat and simmer until water is absorbed, about 25 minutes.

Transfer rice to a large bowl and cool to room temperature.

Combine oil, vinegar, lemon juice, garlic, parsley, salt, and pepper in a small bowl.

Add chicken, shrimp, chorizo, red pepper, tomato, artichoke hearts, peas, green onions, parsley, and olives to rice. Stir to combine, then add enough vinaigrette to lightly coat ingredients. Stir gently, taste, and adjust seasonings if necessary. Refrigerate until serving. Serves 10 to 12.

green onion

Earthy, lemony, and full of healthy goodness, this salad can be a light meal in itself.

CHICKPEA AND TUNA SALAD

19-ounce (540-mL) can chickpeas, drained
¾ cup finely chopped fresh parsley
20 pimiento-stuffed green olives, chopped
4 tablespoons best-quality olive oil
¼ cup fresh lemon juice

7-ounce (198-g) can chunk light or solid white (not flaked) tuna, drained
2 large whole green onions, finely chopped
Salt
Lots of freshly ground black pepper

COMBINE CHICKPEAS, parsley, and olives in a bowl. Add oil and lemon juice.

Break up tuna into large chunks in a small bowl and add to chickpeas. Add green onions, salt, and pepper and stir to combine. Cover and chill for several hours before serving. Taste and adjust seasoning — it should be lemony — if necessary. Serves 4.

WILD AND WHITE RICE SALAD WITH ORANGE ZEST, CURRANTS, AND COCONUT

1⅓ cups wild rice
1⅓ cups basmati or long-grain rice
Grated zest of 2 large oranges
4 large green onions (green part only), finely chopped
1 cup dried currants
3 tablespoons desiccated coconut
¼ cup toasted slivered almonds
½ cup safflower oil
2 tablespoons best-quality olive oil
1 tablespoon Dijon-style mustard
4 tablespoons tarragon vinegar
3 tablespoons dried tarragon

COOK WILD RICE in 4 cups salted water until grains are tender yet still *al dente*, about 30 minutes. If using basmati, rinse the rice under cold water before cooking. Cook white rice in 3 cups water until water is absorbed and rice is tender but not mushy, about 25 minutes. Cool to room temperature.

Toss wild and white rice with orange zest, green onions, currants, coconut, and almonds in a large bowl.

Whisk oils, mustard, vinegar, and tarragon in a small bowl. Drizzle over salad, toss gently, and refrigerate for several hours before serving. Taste and adjust seasoning if necessary. Serves 6 to 8.

B eautiful to look at with its combination of wild and white rice, orange zest, green onions, currants, and coconut. ♦ It is the perfect salad for entertaining, especially as part of a buffet.

Caviar and white beans may seem like an unlikely combination but, believe me, it's utterly divine. ◆ Just perfect as an appetizer, it can be served on both casual and elegant occasions.

White Bean Salad with Caviar

19-ounce (540-mL) can cannellini (white kidney) beans, rinsed and drained

1 medium garlic clove, minced

2 whole green onions, finely chopped

½ cup finely chopped fresh parsley

Grated zest of 1 medium lemon

Lots of freshly ground black pepper

¼ cup best-quality olive oil

2 tablespoons fresh lemon juice

2 teaspoons Dijon-style mustard

Salt

Radicchio leaves

4 ounces lumpfish or salmon caviar

Lemon wedges (garnish)

PLACE BEANS, garlic, green onions, parsley, lemon zest, and pepper in a bowl.

Whisk oil, lemon juice, mustard, and salt in a small bowl and pour over bean mixture. Stir gently to mix and set aside for 30 minutes at room temperature to allow flavors to meld. Do not refrigerate.

Just before serving, line plates with radicchio leaves, top with bean salad, and add a dollop of caviar. Garnish with a wedge of lemon and serve. Serves 4.

TORTELLINI SALAD

1 pound fresh or frozen
green tortellini
(cheese-filled)
1 pound fresh or frozen egg
tortellini (cheese-filled)
2 medium garlic cloves,
minced
¾ cup best-quality olive oil
Grated zest of 1 large lemon
3 tablespoons fresh lemon
juice, or to taste
½ cup freshly grated
Parmesan cheese
4 large whole green onions,
finely chopped

1 cup finely chopped fresh
parsley
1 tablespoon dried basil
10 large sun-dried tomatoes,
drained and cut into
julienne
12 Greek olives (Kalamata),
pitted and quartered
¼ pound good-quality
salami, cut into julienne
Salt
Lots of freshly ground
black pepper

COOK THE TORTELLINI in boiling salted water until *al dente*. Drain and toss with a little oil to prevent sticking. Cool to room temperature.

Combine tortellini, garlic, oil, lemon zest, lemon juice, Parmesan cheese, onions, parsley, basil, sun-dried tomatoes, olives, salami, salt, and pepper in a large bowl. Refrigerate several hours or overnight before serving. Bring back to room temperature before serving. Serves 8 to 10.

ortellini can be purchased at a specialty pasta shop and in some food shops and supermarkets. ♦ Be sure to buy cheese-filled, not meat-filled, tortellini.

ntensely flavored sun-dried tomatoes give their essence to this pasta salad. ◆ *Perfect for picnics and buffets.*

PASTA SALAD WITH SUN-DRIED TOMATOES

1 medium garlic clove
10 large sun-dried tomatoes
  in olive oil, drained
2 large green onions (green
  part only), finely chopped
½ cup finely chopped fresh
  parsley
¼ cup best-quality olive oil
Salt

Lots of freshly ground black
  pepper
¼ cup freshly grated
  Parmesan cheese
½ pound penne, cooked
  until *al dente*, drained,
  and tossed with a little oil
  to prevent sticking

MINCE GARLIC in a food processor. Add sun-dried tomatoes and process until tomatoes become a rough paste.

Toss tomato mixture and green onions, parsley, oil, salt, pepper, and Parmesan cheese with pasta in a large bowl and refrigerate several hours or overnight. Serves 4 to 6.

Tarragon Fusilli Salad

3⅓ cups fusilli, cooked until *al dente*, drained, and rinsed in cold water to cool

1 medium rib celery, finely chopped

1 small onion, finely chopped

1 large sweet red pepper, seeded and cut into ½-inch cubes

⅔ cup mayonnaise

2 to 3 tablespoons rice vinegar

Salt

Lots of freshly ground black pepper

1 tablespoon dried tarragon

COMBINE FUSILLI, celery, onion, red pepper, mayonnaise, vinegar, salt, pepper, and tarragon in a large bowl and refrigerate for several hours before serving. Taste and adjust seasoning if necessary. Serves 4 to 6.

f you love macaroni salad but want something a bit more stylish and elegant, try this one.

New Orleanians are very fond of an Italian sandwich called the Muffuletta. It consists of a 10-inch-round loaf of bread stuffed with salami, cheese, and a mixture known as olive salad. ◆ This spicy, aromatic mixture is not only delicious on sandwiches, it adds a special flavor to tossed green salads and pasta salads like the following.

MUFFULETTA PASTA SALAD

1 medium garlic clove
12-ounce (375-mL) jar pimiento-stuffed green olives, drained
14 Greek olives (Kalamata), pitted
6 marinated artichoke hearts
2 tablespoons sliced hot pickled peppers
1 cup roughly chopped fresh parsley

½ pound small pasta shells, cooked until *al dente*, drained, and tossed with a little oil to prevent sticking
¼ cup best-quality olive oil
2 teaspoons dried oregano
2 tablespoons capers, drained
Salt
Lots of freshly ground black pepper

MINCE GARLIC in a food processor. Add olives, artichokes, hot peppers, and parsley and chop — do not overprocess into a paste. Remove to a large bowl; add pasta and oil, oregano, capers, salt, and pepper. Mix well and refrigerate for several hours or overnight. Serves 8.

CHEESE

SALADS

♦ ♦ ♦

Grainy mustard enlivens this unusual cheese salad. ◆ The Swiss often serve this salad as a first course before Choucroute Garni (a hearty dish of sausages and sauerkraut), but it is also a good accompaniment to grilled or roasted meats.

SWISS CHEESE SALAD WITH GRAINY MUSTARD DRESSING

½ pound Swiss cheese, preferably imported, cut into julienne
2 tablespoons grainy mustard
1 tablespoon red wine vinegar

Salt
½ teaspoon freshly ground black pepper
¼ cup best-quality olive oil
Large handful watercress, large stems removed

TOSS CHEESE with mustard, vinegar, salt, pepper, and oil in a salad bowl. Add watercress and toss again. Serves 4.

WARM GOAT CHEESE SALAD

5 ounces fresh goat cheese, cut in half crosswise, then cut in half
2 tablespoons best-quality olive oil
½ teaspoon dried thyme
Freshly ground black pepper
4 to 6 large lettuce leaves, preferably oakleaf or red leaf lettuce, shredded

¼ cup best-quality olive oil
1 teaspoon Dijon-style mustard
1 teaspoon dried tarragon
2 to 3 teaspoons tarragon vinegar
Salt
Freshly ground black pepper

MARINATE GOAT CHEESE SLICES in oil, thyme, and black pepper for 30 minutes.

Place shredded lettuce in a medium bowl. Combine oil, mustard, tarragon, vinegar, salt, and pepper in a small bowl and pour over lettuce. Toss gently and divide among 4 salad plates.

Heat a small heavy skillet and add goat cheese slices and their marinade. Cook for 15 seconds, then turn and cook another 15 seconds, or until warmed through.

Place cheese slices on top of each salad and serve at once. Serves 4.

nvented in California, marinated chèvre and shredded greens are now a popular item in many restaurants across North America. ♦ *Most chefs use bitter greens such as radicchio, watercress, or arugula and you can, too, if you prefer, but I like the delicacy of leaf lettuce, either red or oakleaf.*

Fresh mozzarella, not the packaged variety, is essential for this salad, as are ripe, flavorful tomatoes, fruity olive oil, and fresh basil. ◆ You may garnish this salad with black olives (Kalamata) as a variation, although it is not traditional.

INSALATA CAPRESE

1 pound fresh mozzarella cheese, sliced ¼-inch thick
3 to 4 medium ripe tomatoes, sliced ¼-inch thick
Chopped fresh basil, to taste

¼ cup best-quality olive oil, or to taste
Balsamic vinegar, to taste
Salt
Freshly ground black pepper

ALTERNATE MOZZARELLA and tomatoes on a serving dish. Sprinkle with basil and drizzle oil and a little vinegar to taste, over top. Salt very lightly and grind a bit of pepper on top. Serve at room temperature. Serves 4 to 6.

INDEX